A PENNY SAVED IS A START...

Memoirs of Rocky Neck

RICHARD VALENTINI

One Printers Way
Altona, MB R0G 0B0
Canada

www.friesenpress.com

Copyright © 2023 by Richard Valentini
First Edition — 2023

All rights reserved.

Photography by Alice M. Valentini

Apologies To Ogden Nash, my version of his poem "Reminiscent Reflection"

No part of this publication may be reproduced in any form, or by any means, electronic or mechanical, including photocopying, recording, or any information browsing, storage, or retrieval system, without permission in writing from FriesenPress.

ISBN
978-1-03-917246-3 (Hardcover)
978-1-03-917245-6 (Paperback)
978-1-03-917247-0 (eBook)

1. BIOGRAPHY & AUTOBIOGRAPHY, PERSONAL MEMOIRS

Distributed to the trade by The Ingram Book Company

DEDICATION

This book of memoirs is dedicated to all of the people that I worked with so long ago at Rocky Neck State Park. In so many ways as compared to today, they had so little but gave so much of themselves. This was especially true in the way they approached their jobs and passed on this positive role model to me.

It is also dedicated to all of the current state park employees who through their ongoing commitment, keep our parks open and create an idyllic place for the public to visit and enjoy. I want to thank all of you for your hard working efforts that many times go unacknowledged.

I also wish to thank all of my fellow teaches, past and present, who have always supported and encouraged me in my efforts to write and finally bring this book to fruition.

CONTENTS

Foreward	1
My Rocky Neck	5
Beach Blanket Bingo	7
A Pennies Worth of Values	13
Meeting the Chicks	23
South Station Boston to Old Saybrook	33
The Honey Wagon	35
Fat Freddie	41
Idiot Sticks	45
Melvin	49
Melvin's Old Sidekick, Eddie	55
"Pennies are a Start" and Mr. Dee	57
The Spy	61
Rocky Neck State Park – a short History	63

Hammonasset – My Plantings of Ivy and Roses	67
My Dad's Summer Memory	75
Mr. Royal	77
Wednesday Off and Janice	83
The Lifeguard War	95
EB Green It	99
The Brush Stroke	105
The Lost *Couga* Caper	109
Hay, a Bundle of Problems?	115
Quebecers, Canucks and Bluenosers	117
Tribute to My Fellow *Nutmeggas*	123
The Tale of the Penny	127
Acknowledgements	133

"WHEN I PONDER HOW MY YOUTH WAS SPENT,
NEVER, EVER DO I CHOOSE REPENT."

APOLOGIES TO OGDEN NASH

FOREWARD

These memoirs are a collection of my coming to age stories told through the lens of over fifty years ago, describing the people, places and my various jobs at a state park in Connecticut. With these tales you'll get insight to the higher expectations and demands adults had for the youth of that era. We were considered to be just like the older employees, treated like adults and not just teenage children. We followed much stricter social mores and codes of behavior than young people experience today. We lived in a society that was shaped more by our elder's experiences than by the technological explosion and revolution caused by the ever present social media and the demand of immediate self-gratification.

Learning to accept responsibility, being held accountable for my actions made me more able to deal with and overcome future adversities later in life. This was also my intent to praise and thank the people who unknowingly helped by giving me many of life's survival skills and helped to shape my life as I know it today. This is what my collection of memoirs is all about. I hope you enjoy them as much as I enjoyed putting my memories in writing.

And now you can begin reading. Just keep looking for some of the penny stories included in some of these pages and examine the coin change in your hand. Each penny like us has a story unto itself.

I hope you find some of my old hidden pennies with your next Rocky Neck visit and but mainly to remember to value and appreciate everything that you have. We forget that most of the world has to do without so many of the items that we take for granted.

I also realize that we have a finite amount of time on this Earth. That we only have a short amount of time that we are able to remember and to write about our life. It's like trying to hold water in your hand. It only lasts for a moment. You need to do the things to achieve your goals, accomplishing it before you give up or you create an excuse why it never gets done. If I had put these ideas and writings on the bookshelf, it would never have gotten completed or printed.

When I write about the penny, it's not about the value of the penny itself. It's the concept that most small, unnoticed everyday items you possess or ideas you have can be the start of a better life. This is what working at Rocky Neck taught me and what I want to pass on to you.

Rich Valentini

Ellie Mitchell Pavilion 10/2022

MY ROCKY NECK

Depression era stone masons built
    this huge pavilion,
Still one of the largest public structures
    in our state – Connecticut.
So sturdy, this Ellie Mitchell building should
    last until oblivion.

Feel the hard, cold boulders, with soft shoulders,
    take in its massive weight.
Picture wiry, strong as granite men, hauling, lifting,
    laboring with their fast paced gait.
These sturdy hearted New Englander males
    and females,
        driving, directing, caring and cooking,
All so this park and its massive pavilion could
    be great.

Constructing this monument with fortitude
    and hope,
        by those who would soon be marching off
        to war.

All hands joined in together so their spirits could soar.
Those now long gone Yankees who conquered
> their fears,
> to give us a place that will forever endure.

This great fortress of glacial stone,
> but no cannons here found,
Always welcomes me home.
In the nutmeg state, it's my favorite place,
> and rules over Long Island Sound!

R. Valentini

DARN STORY AND POEMS

I really don't care for novels and poems,
> But for you Rich, what the heck,
> > I'll read your darn story,
> > > about Rocky Neck.
Hmmm . . . so far so good.
I like what I've read. It kept me up,
> When I should've been in bed.

R. Valentini

BEACH BLANKET BiNGO

Connecticut's Rocky Neck sits on land that the state set aside where people who can't afford to live next to the Long Island Sound can enjoy the beach for a day. No one can evict them for trespassing, as it's owned by the state.

The smell of salt water, suntan lotion, and fried food filled the air, along with the screeching by seagulls and kids yelling and tugging at their moms. The kids saying things like, "When can we go in the water? Is that a jellyfish? I'm hungry. I have to go to the bathroom!"

Of course everyone had brought their own radio, sitting at the edge of their beach blanket. Each turned the volume up for all to hear. I still have my old 1967 Arvin AM FM radio and it still works. It was my prized possession and cost a total of $18 new. That was big bucks back then.

In my mind, I can still hear the jingle, "Come On, Over," on both my transistor and car radio, to go to visit the now long gone, Palisades Amusement Park in New Jersey. It was written by Gladys Shelley (c) 1965 and sung by Steve Clayton.

It was a great radio jingle and you can listen to it on U Tube. I don't need to listen to it as I know the words by heart, even after all these years. It is one of those great ear worms that is still stuck in my brain. I can hear that jingle playing every time I visit a beach, especially Rocky Neck.

I'm sure those of you who went to the beach in that era know the tune. It filled the radio waves and I heard it every time I turned on my favorite radio stations while driving my car. Thanks for the great commercial Gladys. I would have liked to talk to her about her writing it but she passed in 2003.

The jingle remained the amusement park's theme song from 1965 until 1971 when Palisades Amusement Park closed. Ironically, what I didn't know until doing this research was that Gladys wrote the jingle for her husband who owned the park. Again, thanks for the memory Gladys, of a jingle that comes to mind whenever I smell the salt water of the ocean.

I remember listening to my favorite rock and roll stations, blaring the top ten hits. Either New York's WABC with disk jockey "Cousin Brucie," or WINS

"Murray the K," with even more brain worm commercials that I can hear even now.

Everywhere, on a good summer day, thousands of multi- colored umbrellas and beach blankets filled every inch of beach space. With so many blankets, it looked like people hanging out laundry or a big rug sale in Turkey. It was a miracle not to be stepped on by someone; like living in a can of sardines but at the beach.

My mother hated sand getting on her blanket, or us getting her hair wet when she tried to swim in the ocean. But, she loved the beaches, Rocky Neck and Ocean Beach. Ocean Beach was too far to drive to as we now lived in East Lyme, so Rocky Neck become her new favorite beach.

I missed the Boardwalk, the pools to swim in, Pinball and Skee Ball machines in the Gam and the carnival rides at Ocean Beach, but I enjoyed the ocean best of all and what a great beach we had with Rocky Neck! We went to Rocky Neck, Monday through Friday and sometimes, if my Dad was willing, we'd go on a Saturday or Sunday too. At Rocky Neck, during low tide, you felt like you could walk out, all the way across to Long Island or even a bit further to England.

It's no wonder I still love going to beaches. My wife Alice and I have a small cottage in Madison and I go biking and swimming right across the Boston Post Road to Hammonasset Beach, the state park to the west of Rocky Neck, every day to swim if I can.

Though I now live thousands of miles away in California, I can still hear the sounds of the beach - the gentle surf, and the noise of the arriving crowds of people eager to have fun. The smell of the ocean and family cookouts come to my senses. I feel the hot sand on my feet, transporting me back to the beach in those days, as if it was yesterday.

MY NEW ENGLAND SHORE SERENADE

First you see the gulls, feel the breeze and hear
    the surf,
Your mind unwinds with every sand filled step,
Walking the beach is so unlike your normal turf,
Where your memories coming like gentle waves of
    the past are kept.
Trips to Ocean Beach and Rocky Neck, the happiest
    of times,
Even though I'm miles away are clearly in my mind.

Then I say in my best New England chant:
"I should hope to shout *louda*,
Fried clams and *chowda*,
Cup a *lobsta* bisque within my reach,
As I go to the store to buy some *beeah*,
And drive *ova* to Rocky Neck's beach."

R. Valentini

A PENNiES WORTH OF VALUES

Pennies you find in Rocky Neck are magical. How do I know this you ask? Oh, I know this to be true.

I still have the penny I found at Rocky Neck in the summer of '69. It's an old, real copper one from 1962 and it helped to get me through the best and worst of times. I kept it, but threw back another one in the park to take its place. I have pennies still hidden in Rocky Neck. You just have to know where to look. Maybe I'll help you find them or I can just let my old penny friends stay where they are, nice and snug from so long ago. Pennies are a start, as you'll find out.

Once, when I worked in the old stone pavilion, the building you can spot on Google Maps. It's so big! We were unloading some materials for repair. I thought, I'll put some pennies in the stone wall ramp at the end of the driveway. No one will ever find them there and someday, I'll come back to retrieve them, or somebody will have fun finding them. I stuck a few into the small stone crevices between the big wall boulders, and slid some in where the cement had worn away.

I'm sure, no one has brought a metal detector up to that wall. I pushed those pennies further back with a Popsicle stick to be out of the elements of rain, frost and snow. Maybe they're not all green with oxidation. My poor, old Abe. I wonder if his beard has grown even longer in all that time?

They have to be there I believe, even after forty-three years. I'll check it out this fall when I visit (unless you beat me to it) and put them back in the same spot. Of course, I'll make a point of adding a few more.

Rich at Ellie Mitchell Pavilion 10/2022

STONE SPIRITS

> The ghost of my past,
> Resides inside this rock wall,
> Though my life's now recast,
> My name it still recalls.
>
> R. Valentini

If you ever find a penny at Rocky Neck, keep it, make a wish and throw back another penny if you have one, so someone else can find it and make a wish too. Or just keep that magical penny for yourself. I won't tell anyone.

Finding one of those pennies, also guarantees that, sometime in your future, you'll make another safe journey back to Rocky Neck. It could be ten, twenty, thirty, forty or some cases fifty years later or more, but you will return. It's kind of like our own Trevi Fountain in Rome, but this time it's in Connecticut, a short drive for some people and you only have to throw the penny in a field or hide one in a stone wall. Better do it before they quit making that lowly, but lovely little penny.

At the entrance to the park you drive around a field waiting in line to pay your entrance fee. If you are a Connecticut resident you can just drive through. Only people with out of state license plates pay. When driving through, make a wish and please throw a penny out the window. I always call it the Mr. Dee field, after my old work buddy. Hopefully, you too will find another penny somewhere in the park and have double the good fate. Throw one and later try to find one.

I threw lots of pennies out of my car, motorcycle, or bike for all four summers when I was working there. I still throw pennies out my car window when I visit and it has always brought me back home safe and sound. I'm sure it will work the same for you too. So again, throw out that penny and make a wish! Mr. Dee will take off his hat, rub his bald head and smile down on you. A penny for your thoughts, Mr. Dee. Although these memoirs are not just about pennies and mostly about the people at Rocky Neck, I can't help but think how important these coins seem to be, especially to me and hopefully in the future to you.

Reading onward, you'll see how finding and keeping pennies played a role while I worked at Rocky Neck. Important lessons learned when a penny could be a valued item. Also to value not just objects like these and our other inanimate possessions, but instead to value people. To value our former classmates, friends and family members which now in many cases have passed on.

This is true when I see most younger people today, having to learn what I did at a much earlier age, that you should appreciate what you have. That's another reason why I wrote these memoirs, that hopefully you will get the feeling of the era, personalities and life's lessons learned.

We will, I'm sure, quit minting coins and printing paper money as we know it today. But until that time happens, I will continue to pick up someone's errant penny because to me it represents not just the one cent but the value of something bigger in life, something that an elder, whom I greatly admired, taught me so long ago. That everything, no matter how small has a value unto itself. So I pick up the pennies I find today, and each time thank my Rocky Neck buddies for showing me the way to live a good productive life. In reading these stories I hope you will feel the same way too and experience what I learned and appreciate things in life both big and small.

When I see people buy some small items at convenience stores, a majority of them only use their debt cards. I don't own a debit card. I think that by using cash it gives me a better idea of the cost of an object and what exactly I'm spending because I can see the transaction.

Some of these debit card users, I'm sure, think of money, dollars, coins and especially pennies as a thing of the past and a nuisance. But, by using cash and coins, you get to add, subtract, multiply, and divide, use fractional parts, etc. You know exactly what your money is buying. That's the math teacher in me I guess. I like to think, what is the cost, is it on sale and can I get a better deal elsewhere? Again, the math teacher at work.

When I get some change back, especially pennies, I love to look at the dates. I think, what I was doing that year the coin was minted? Where was I going? It's like I'm holding a little history. I still have some of the pennies I found so long ago at Rocky Neck. I wonder who held these older coins? What was going on in that person's mind at the time? I wish these coins could speak. Was this person going off to war, getting something for the person they loved or helping out their family in some way? Maybe someone famous has held one of these coins long ago. Who knows?

People may think of this as silly, remembering the past through pennies but pennies and the stories they created have helped me write some of these memories which in turn gave me the title.

I hope that pennies are never gotten rid of, or at least not in my lifetime, like it has in our neighbor to the north, Canada. You want the pennies minted before 1982. These are 95% copper and 5% zinc. A 1981 penny is now worth 2.2 cents, so finding one has already doubled your money. Another reason for using cash and checking your penny change.

In 1633 George Herbert published in *Outlandish Proverbs*, "a penny spar'd is twice got." Then in 1737 our countryman, Benjamin Franklin, wrote in *Poor Richards Almanac*, "a penny saved is two pence clear," which he later wrote as "a penny saved is a penny earned."

Think of all the other penny phrases and sayings that we've heard all our lives, and perhaps add:

"It's not worth a red cent," "put my two cents in," "I'll give you a penny for your thoughts," the penny arcade, penny candy, penny loafers, (shoes, not people), penny gumball machines (no longer found, I guess), and to "penny-ante," (not much to risk or bet). All of these idiomatic expressions have helped shape our opinions concerning that little penny both good and bad. They show the effect that this small coin has had on our lives.

A math teacher that writes? Uncanny you say? Well, a penny found is a start, as my old friend would say. Reading on, you will meet an assortment of people and learn of my activities while working those summers long ago at Rocky Neck.

"Hey, it's not my fault, I'm only summer help." This was the standard response all the time from us part timers during the four summers I worked there. We said it when things didn't work or were broken, even if it was our fault. You never heard "awesome," "I'm good," "no worries," or "yeah . . . right." We were much more expressive, probably to the dismay of our friends, co-workers and employers. "Put that in your pipe and smoke it" or "kid, put an egg in your shoe and beat it." "You egg suckin' dog." Aren't those sayings a little more interesting and colorful? I think we had a better command of the language. We read more and viewed electronics less, that's for sure!

So let's get on with some of the park people, the park stories and my personal stories. Hang on tightly, here comes the first dip in this rocky road.

MEETiNG THE CHiCKS

Slowly walking down on the heavily forested road that took me away from Storrs, where the University of Connecticut is located. I carried my parents old 1940's maroon and tan suitcase. My head down, feeling full of remorse, dragging one foot ahead of the other; me, another hapless teenager trying to figure out which road in life to take.

I had just had my father drop me off earlier that afternoon at UCONN, that large campus in northeast Connecticut.

I had repeatedly called and spoken with a girl I was enamored with, named Janice, and was hoping to get a chance to see her before I returned to college that fall.

My dad had turned around his Rust-Oleum painted grey, '65 Volkswagen Bug and left. He drove back to our home in East Lyme after I told him I'd just take the bus to Hartford and then on to my college, at Western Connecticut State in Danbury. "It's ok,

Dad," I said, "I'll call you in Danbury when I find the nearest phone booth."

Walking around and finding her dorm, I asked at the front desk if Janice could come out for a visit but another young girl came down and said she wasn't available. Didn't she know I was coming? After all I had left a message for her. Stunned, I didn't know what to say. Mumbling, I just said ok and left. I felt like such a fool to assume that I could just show up and see her. Now what do I do? Maybe she was out? I just figured she didn't want to see me. So, looking back on it now, instead of considering the other options she might have taken or where else she could have been, I just gave up and walked out totally dejected. I guess that was when I realized my four years of fun times with Janice were over, just like the end of my four years of summer employment at the state park at Rocky Neck where we had both worked together.

The people, all the crazy jobs I had, the voices of each person, the laughter, New England accents, like "Hey *chowda* head." The agony of hard physical work but then again, mostly fun – all came to an end. At the end of those four brief summers, I never saw any of those people again. Whether any of these people are still alive, I don't know; hopefully they are and this will rekindle in their minds our great antics and the memories of that time in our collective history.

The few times over the years when I do visit the park, I'm always disappointed my old co-workers don't appear, even though it's been some fifty years. I'd love to go back to those times again, even if only for a day. But of course, time doesn't stand still, the only place it stands still is in your mind.

Just think of those times: there were no electronic addictions - cell phones, computers, texting, emojis, laptops, or streaming, unless in the water, all of us clamming. It was a truly kinder and gentler time. The unfortunate now common "F" word was not in use by anyone. People weren't wearing ball caps backwards or forwards. No scruffy beards. No tattoos were seen except on sailors, or body piercings, or dyed hair, or especially that atrocious flaming red hot color. We were expected to dress and act appropriately. Proper haircuts and wearing trousers with belts, no shorts or sandals to work. These were the unspoken dress codes. No sloppy attire was ever seen on any employee and we always addressed people in charge with a respectful Mr., Mrs., Sir, or Ma'am. We represented our park and our state with pride.

We all lived in what I considered were the best of times, only we didn't know it back then. We lived in a time that those of us who are still alive, realize, proves we can live without any of those distracting electronic devices and still enjoy all that life has to offer. I say this about a lot of the kids today fifty years later, always staring at their phones. They know the price of everything but the value of nothing. These are my own observations.

We were the teenagers of the Sixties. Our folks didn't bail us out of any problems we encountered or made excuses for us if we didn't like our jobs or our current place in life. No one cared if we had a headache and child anxiety didn't exist as far as we knew. We were taught that if you took on something, like a job or a project, you finished it. If you lost a game, you lost, no consolation prize was given. You always had tomorrow to improve. Nothing in life was all about you and what you wanted. If you had some problem, no one really cared. And the world news of nuclear war and the Vietnam Conflict was always hanging over our heads like an ogre waiting to strike.

"You are a teenager," they said, "How could you have a problem?" You had no bills to pay or a house payment. Bruised egos were not allowed, you simply forgot about it and moved on.

We took verbal abuse from some people, learned to suck it up and also at times how to give it right back and stick up for ourselves. Showing up to work on time and working hard all day was the way we earned the most respect from people. We understood the grind of daily work and admired the men and women who did just that, day in and day out. Those were the people we wanted to emulate.

All of these early life experiences have stayed with me making me a better person. I learned to make the best of every situation and to laugh at myself. To find humor in most things in life and never hold a grudge. As they say, "grudges are too heavy and they don't have handles."

It helped me later on in life when I decided to become a teacher, to become an even better one. Even though I was a young age, I felt my work and life experiences made me much better able to handle difficult situations and people; much more so than someone else my own age. Maybe that's why when I became a teacher, I never experienced teacher burn out. I was used to hard, demanding work and didn't need a pat on the back for doing what I was hired to do. My jobs at Rocky Neck played a huge role in creating that way of thinking.

I taught mostly special education kids over my long teaching career; holding them to the same standards and behavior as I did any other student.

I would use the same educational materials as the regular classrooms; I wanted them to be treated with the same dignity and respect as anyone else. This I required from other teachers, other students and the parents of the special education students as well.

Back to the times at Rocky Neck and what a roller coaster ride it was! Full of ups and downs, like the big Cyclone coaster at Coney Island. But first, back to my misadventure.

Thinking there was a Greyhound station at Storrs, I was wrong! I set out walking south down old Route 44 to Hartford, about 30 miles, knowing at least there was a Greyhound station for me there in downtown Hartford.

Crying, both ashamed and mad at myself for being such an idiot, I quickly realized how heavy that old suitcase was. No car, little money, and no visit with Janice. Not only no way to talk to her, but unable to talk to anyone. No phone booths on this stretch of road that I could see. But who would I call and what would I say? It was better to just keep walking.

Thinking that this day couldn't get any worse, and of course, before I could spit, it did. And, I should hope to shout - it started raining! It quickly got damp and cold, the weather resembling my crappy mood.

Putting my suitcase over my head to shield me a little and looking down at my soaking feet, I started laughing at my situation. God, I didn't believe that was happening. My feet began to squeak like I was stepping on little mice.

Was I going the right way? Yes, there's a sign, Manchester twenty miles ahead. Ok Rich, I thought, just keep walking. You can't get any wetter. And what a slight I must have been, looking like a drowned rat in the middle of nowhere, way out here in East Jesus, the boonies of Connecticut. I had to somehow get to Hartford and then on to Danbury where I went to college, "Hat City," as it was also known back then. Should I hitchhike? Hmmm . . yes, that's a good idea! I stuck out my thumb and hoped for the best.

As the cars and trucks raced by, with the water splashing up on me from every vehicle, I thought who's going to pick up this wet as a dishrag kid, with a suitcase stuck on his head? But, before I knew it, a guy pulled his truck over and asked me where I was going. I told him Hartford and he told me to jump in. Not in the cab mind you, his daughter was already sitting there, but in the bed of the truck.

He had an old faded door emblem with of some type of animal painted on the truck. I had no idea what the animal emblem was until I got in the truck bed. And what an unpleasant surprise it was!

The truck bed had a tarp synched over the top of it. I opened the rear flap and jumped up and in. My feet were already tired and it felt good, to just sit. Only now, instead of sitting with the one chick at UCONN I wanted to see, I was now sitting there with a bunch of caged chickens. I went from no chick to excess chicks.

These chickens were being brought up the road to Wethersfield to some hatchery. Squawking, screeching, pecking each other and at me, with feathers flying and manure spreading all over, my elegant coach took off for my first destination, Hartford. At least I wasn't getting any wetter.

After what seemed like forever and getting good at holding my breath from the stench, we got near Hartford. I hopped out by a Howard Johnsons Restaurant, thanked the driver and his daughter for the ride, said goodbye to my new found hens and walked downtown toward the bus station. Still wet, feet soaked and shoes squeaking; I was cold, hungry and tired. As I walked into the Greyhound station, I wondered why are people staring at me and giggling?

Not only did I have a trail of water following me, but stuck on my back and on the rear of my pants were various sized feathers and chicken droppings! I was like Moses parting the Red Sea. Everyone suddenly moved apart to give me a seat! It was like I was tarred and feathered, or had a big "F" for fowl, written on my chest. I'm sure, for even the people reading their newspapers, my smell made them jerk their heads and sit erect.

Needless to say, no one sat next to me on the bus either and I sat in silence through all the Greyhound stops in New Britain, Waterbury, and what seemed like every small town in western Connecticut, on the way to my final destination, Danbury. I stared outside, watching the rain run down the window and rubbed the steam and moisture off with my feathered elbow. I could have passed for a foul rooster. What a miserable day this was.

I began thinking about my times at the park, with Janice, Fred, Melvin, Eddie, Mr. Dee, Mr. Royal and all the other eclectic assortment of people I worked with there. They all have a special place in my heart as you can see by my writing. I'm trying to rekindle and download my thoughts before it all disappears.

SOUTH STATION BOSTON TO OLD SAYBROOK

Today, the Amtrak coach, which left South Boston Station on train #93, whizzes past my favorite Connecticut beach, Rocky Neck. With my wife Alice and I on board the train, a cascade of memories float through my mind. A kaleidoscope of the past. My brain flickers with each view, like an old black and white news reel.

Although my memory seems to be gently fading from that time, some fifty plus years ago, I can't help but smile and chuckle to myself as I look out the window and hear the train agent say, "Next stop, Old Saybrook." I'm thinking, can we please go slower past my old haunt, Rocky Neck?

I know in that ten seconds, as we pass Rocky Neck heading west, those memories have given me the pages of stories and tales of people's lives for this book. I hope you enjoy them as much as I enjoy remembering them. Great times, and I consider myself lucky to have grown up in a different era, as a young man at a lovely Connecticut Park. Rocky Neck, summer employment, 1968-71, how could it be any better??

But let me continue with some of the characters and tales.

THE HONEY WAGON

My first year at the park in 1968, I got the job pushing around an old wooden cart with two wheels, called the "Honey Wagon." I soon found out, it had nothing to do with honey, and it wasn't really a wagon. It was like an old push cart the old Italians used to sell vegetables and fish from on the lower East Side of New York City in the 1920's. With two large wheels in the front, you had to lift the front to make it move. It was unwieldy, bulky and heavy; painted green with the words "Honey Wagon" painted on the side.

I had no idea what it meant, but I soon found out. My new job was to clean all of the outhouses at the camp ground. Living the dream job I guess! Oh well, I had a summer job and was making a cool $1.85 an hour!

The Honey Wagon had a large pole attached to the side of it, scrub brushes, some kind of state designated liquid cleaner and the folding type of toilet paper that went into those locked, small metal receptacles. There were no flush toilets at the camp ground back then. The flushing mechanism was me. I had to take one of the two long poles and push the human waste down into the septic tank way down below, clean the seat and the whole toilet stall, check the toilet tissue supply and move on.

After a while, the two poles smelled like human feces and I had to spray them and my long gloves with a hose nozzle about three or four times a day. I had about forty outhouses to pump and clean plus some of the new porta-potties at various places inside the campgrounds. It was a breathtaking experience.

It took me most of the day and no one really bothered me. I was kind of an attraction at the park and people wanted to take my picture. I started to get to know all of the campers and all of the campground gossip; like who was zooming who? That's how I met Janice, the girl who was to be my four summer flame and her parents. I was such great outhouse catch.

On the fourth of July, some of the campers got drunk. They got into a fight about I know not what and that night, they set some of the outhouses on fire! The outhouses were made of wood and went up like Roman candles. I wasn't there that night but at least four were set ablaze and were totaled.

The next day the fire engines were still at the park. The park rangers never did find out who set them on fire. In a way, I thought it was funny. Maybe the campers were tired of those old septic holes in the ground, but I, at least, had four less outhouses to clean.

My last year at the park, regular flush toilets and hot showers were installed. To me though, that isn't what I call camping. Camping to me, is to learn to rough it a little, come on, don't be such a snowflake. Wake up to the smell of a warm canvas tent with crusty eye boogers on your face and your clothes having the odor of burnt wood. Now, that's camping.

I think the state of Connecticut was having to compete with some local private campgrounds and knew they had to upgrade the facilities. Damnit, no more Honey Wagon after 1971.

I always wore long pants working the Honey Wagon, even though it was hot. I also wore my Rocky Neck State Park T-shirt and a jaunty brimmed hat. In the hat's band, I had a large seagull feather sticking out of it and of course my Sixties buttons: one was the peace sign, one that said "Draft Beer not Students" and my favorite, "Support Mental Health or I'll Kill You!" Funny at the time, but of course you'd probably be crucified for that today.

Phil was my boss and he ran the campground at Rocky Neck. All the camping site reservations went through him. No reservations were made online back then. Online was where I hung my clothes.

Phil chain smoked Viceroys like a fiend, and I could never relax inside the campground office because it was like being in a large ashtray and all my clothes would later reek of cigarette smoke. When people came inside to inquire about a camping site, he'd say, "First come first serve." and if someone asked about the type of toilets we had there, Phil would hold up a shovel to the usual gasp of some new female camper.

Then he explained the type of septic toilets we had and pointed to me, and said, ask the "Honey Wagon" man, Rich, if you have any problems. There were showers too, but no hot water, only very cold water during the summer months. But then again you were camping.

The problem with being in charge of the Honey Wagon was that the other park employees and part-time workers would razz me. One of the older, permanent maintenance workers, Melvin started to call me "Stink," a moniker that lasted for three summers, long after I didn't have the job as the camp janitor at the campground. Much to my dismay, he had everyone calling me "Stink."

I had to tell them it was about the first job I had at the park, not me personally and that Melvin didn't care for college students to boot. Melvin seemed to take pleasure in calling me "Stink." I started calling Melvin a name I will mention later and the following year I started working mostly with Mr. Dee.

While being in charge of the Honey Wagon, I got to know the campers and how they lived. I learned about the daily lives of those who stayed on for long-term camping. I learned how they kept their jobs and took care of their permanent homes elsewhere and I got to witness all the campground upgrades in those fast four summers.

The campground went from primitive to modern in a flash, but then again, as I quickly learned about everything else in life, everything changes, whether you're ready for it or not.

I was the last of the great Honey Wagon employees. Could I put that on a future resume? Job experience: A real crackerjack at emptying human waste and refuse. "Yes, let's hire him. It sounds like he's a real champion at wasting time."

FAT FREDDiE

Fred, an assistant ranger, worked at the park most of the summers I did. He was a fire chief in the town Niantic, the main town on the coast of East Lyme. I went to school and graduated with his daughter, Barbara, who was very pretty and she still is to this day. Fred never knew I knew his daughter, not that it would have made a difference.

Fred was a big man, heavy set, an anomaly, not like today. In fact, I can't remember anyone back then, in the Sixties, being heavy set. Everyone seemed normal size or thin. I was always like a short pencil!

Fred walked with a lumbering gait, a side to side motion and he tugged at his pants a lot. In the corner of his mouth was planted a short cigar, a "guinea stinker," we used to call it. An offensive slang for an Italian cigar.

Fat Freddie always had a park uniform on and rode around the park on a little white Honda 50cc motorcycle. It was a scene that looked like a huge elephant riding on a tricycle in the circus. When he got on that poor motorcycle, the seat disappeared under his girth. Every time he got on it, I groaned under my breath for that poor tiny machine.

I was one of the maintenance guys, the lowest of the low on the totem pole of jobs at the park, a real bottom feeder. Part-time summer help earning money, first while in high school and then earning money for college.

For four summers I worked there and learned a lot about life, jobs and people that helped me experience life situations. It was all about learning good employment skills and all part of the human comedy of my life. I hope as you read, you will laugh or cry with me and enjoy reminiscing about the past as much as I do. Now, back to Fat Freddie.

I never called Fred, "Fat Freddie," to his face. I thought it would be pretty rude to do that to an adult, but that is what he was he was known as behind his back.

While I was cleaning up the beach and idiot sticking around one of the ranger stations one Monday, Fat Freddie yelled out at me, "Hey you, Valentini, come in here."

"What's the matter Fred?" I asked.

"There's a bat stuck in the screen in my window and I need you to take your idiot stick and kill it. I'm petrified of bats." he said. I thought to myself, so what? Why do I have to do it? Geez, this has been the story of my life.

I took my idiot stick, gently lifted up the glass window inside of the screen and slowly impaled the bat with the nail on the end of the broom stick handle, i e. an idiot stick. And I was the resident idiot using one.

"Great," Fred said. "Take that damn thing out and make sure it's dead!"

With the bat still flopping and stuck on my nail point, I went outside and gave the bat an extra thrust with the point of the nail, saw the blood on the bat's mouth and it went limp. "OK, Fred", I said, "It's done, dead." Gross, I thought.

"Is the screen ok?" he asked. "You didn't put a hole in it did you?"

"No, there's just some bat blood," I replied.

"Thanks," Fred said. Then he went back to yelling to someone from his fire department on what we called his "bitch box." This "bitch box," was a two-way radio connection to his office in Niantic, a walkie-talkie; a kind of primitive cell phone. Along with that ubiquitous cigar always stuck on the corner of this mouth, the bitch box was always stuck in his ear.

As I was off to do some beach cleanup, my reason for being there in the first place, Fred removed his hand off his bitch box receiver and said, "Oh, by the way, call your mom up when you find a phone somewhere. Something happened at your home. I think your grandfather passed away or something."

That's how I found out my Dad's dad, my grandfather, Ricardo, had had a heart attack and passed away. I couldn't find a phone until the end of my day shift. Thank God I had a dime in my pocket to use on a pay phone outside the park at a nearby motel.

My mom answered, "Yes, it's true," she stated bluntly, "Grandad had a heart attack and died. Are you finally on your way home? Hurry, if you can."

Before I could answer, she hung up.

IDIOT STICKS

I've mentioned idiot sticks before, and some of you may not recall of what I speak. Please, read further.

An idiot stick is a broom handle that has a nail pounded into one end and the flat nail head grounded off on a lathe in the shop to a fine point. Today you would use a grabber stick. Stab the garbage and put it into the garbage cans. Simple, easy, I could make idiot sticks and knew what they were for. A true born idiot *sticka*.

"Alright you summer help," Al said with his stammer and stutter. "Today you will clean up the *paak* after our busy weekend. Take an idiot stick and grind up the point and get in one of the trucks!" "And check on those port-a-potties outside the *paak*."

The port-a-potties or outhouses outside the main road into Rocky Neck were known to every employee at the park as the magnificent seven. I don't know if they still exist today. I hope not.

Al was one of the foremen at the park. Nice guy, he had never been married and called the women's hygiene sanitary napkin we placed in the outhouses or port- a -potties, "a motex". This was his awkward combination of Modess and Kotex, two feminine hygiene product names.

We all died laughing when he said that and Al would turn beet red and would stammer even more. "You know what I mean!" he said with a bluster, "Those girlie things."

The unofficial name for those nasty port-a -potties was "Polish spaceships" as the old timers would say or sometimes just an outhouse. I just called them Melvin's lockers. In the heat of the summer they really exuded a fragrant stench.

We piled into the back of a truck, an older, noisy Ford dump truck and took off to the beach.

Inside the truck bed it was hot, smelled of garbage but we yelled and sang some Rolling Stones tunes and swung our idiot sticks at the passing tree leaves while riding to the edge of the park. No bottled water, no snacks, no cell phones to stare at, or earbuds stuck in our ears to listen to.

We only had each other and I quickly learned to not do what was called "piss and moan," or complaining.

But for some older workers, pissing and moaning was a hobby, and lucky for them I was a quick study.

But the full-time employees rarely complained, and if they did it was legit and concerned safety and better working conditions. They had no union to represent them for wages and benefits as far as I knew, so they stuck together and voiced united opinions. These men and women knew what hard work was and seemed happy to be employed.

When the full time employees complained about anything, it was mostly about us summer help kids and not much else. To them we could be late, lazy, sloppy and ignorant of most things – some of which were true.

Using idiot sticks, Rocky Neck. That's me on the left 1971.

MELViN

Melvin was one of our older truck drivers who worked full time for the park service. He was from Norwich and had collected tons of boxes of arrowheads and other various Indian artifacts from the Thames River in Eastern Connecticut. Or so he said.

"Just go down to the river's edge and there's tons of signs of the Mohegan Indians who lived there for thousands of years." Melvin would state. However, he never brought any Native American items to work, but talked about them all the time.

He didn't like all the people crowding in at the beach, the mess they left for us to clean up or us young college kids that he had to put up with.

Melvin was the one who started to call me "Stink" after my first job at the park, but that's a later chapter. It took him four summers to finally call me by my first name. In my first year there, he could be a pain in the ass, constantly razzing me. In turn I called him "Smellvin." Nobody else called him "Smellvin," except me but on the other hand lots of people started to call me "Stink." Thanks Melvin.

In the truck cab, when you weren't looking he'd punch your knee hard with his fist and then laugh like a crazy man. What a gentle sense of humor he had.

If it was ten o'clock, no matter if we were driving, working on a building or having a garbage run, we had to stop for coffee time. Ten o'clock coffee time was the rule. If not, Melvin would throw a hammer or shovel at you!!

"It's ten o'clock, coffee time," he'd say, and we all sat for a break, which actually was nice. As long as you missed the hammer throw.

One time, Melvin took us to some kind of job to do at another state park called Gillette Castle. It was the former home of an actor and playwright, William Gillette and was built in 1919.

The castle is called the Seventh Sister, after the seven nearby hills and looked like a castle the Vikings would have like to storm. It wasn't too far away, sat north of us on the east side of the Connecticut River, but I had never been there.

We got our crew together and all the necessary tools, electrical wire, pipes, pipe cutters, hammers, screws, nails, shovels and bags of cement. I had no idea what the job would entail.

We finally got the truck loaded and left Rocky Neck late. In the front sat Melvin, Eddie and Mr. Dee. I sat in the bed of the truck with a couple of other summer help guys, Pete and Dennis.

It was hot in the bed of those trucks but we were young and could take it. None of the truck cabs had any air conditioning back then anyway, better to be out in the fresh air and away from the three guys inside and their constant cigarette smoke.

As we got on the road it was close to ten o'clock and Melvin stopped the truck because it was coffee time. After a half an hour or so we started up again. Then we had to stop somewhere to get gas!

By the time we arrived at the castle it was almost lunch and Melvin and the full timers were not ones who missed their lunch. So we all sat down and ate. I didn't want to have to duck a Melvin hammer throw.

After lunch we went up to the park ranger there to see what needed to be fixed and it was only a small section of rock stairway.

But we had brought no rocks or stone slabs. As you may well know, Connecticut's soil is full of rocks, so we ambled down to the river's edge and started digging with picks and shovels.

I somehow fell into the river or was pushed. I got out and pulled another one of the guys in and before you knew it we were all wet! It was a hot, humid day and we were having some fun.

Melvin finally said "Ok boys, that's enough." We each took a large rock back up the steep hill to the stairway. We wedged them into where we thought they would fit, mixed up some cement and sand, then we poured it around the rocks.

After about one hour, the work was completed. It wasn't very difficult. I don't know why so many people were needed but back then there was no way to double check on a work order. You took what you thought you needed and hoped for the best. Oh well, like I said we had a lot of fun at a different park. We laughed all the way back to Rocky Neck. All that travel and time for only an hour's work! We were never sent back to Gillette's Castle again.

Another time we had to put up "No Clamming" signs on the east end of the park at Rocky Neck, in a brackish stream. Now, I don't remember if the clams were supposed to be bad for eating or if it was a stream where the clams were being seeded. I do know that after we put the signs up, Melvin took off his shoes, rolled up his sleeves and his pant legs and got a small shovel and started digging for clams.

Soon, we all had our shoes and socks off, rolled up our pants and were clam digging. Eddie, Mr. Dee, and some other summer help guys were with us that day. Melvin sent me to drive back to our maintenance shop where I retrieved more buckets to put our catch in and more small shovels to dig up our clams. And what a catch it was! We spent the whole day in that stream clamming.

Melvin told the curious passerby walking to the beach, "Oh no, we weren't clamming, not with those signs up. We were just taking in some clams to check to see if they had red tide. They research all of these diseases now. We didn't want anyone to get sick or anything." Melvin never met a corner he didn't cut.

There was no red tide and I'm sure the state was trying to preserve a clam bed, where clams could develop. We didn't help it any, though. But we all had a bucket of clams to take home at the end of the day.

No one was the wiser and we never mentioned it to anyone. Melvin gave us all a big wink before he took off in his car and we had another fun day with him in charge. Thanks Melvin for the great memory!

Melvin hated the development going on in Connecticut way back in 1969. He'd get out his Thermos of coffee, light a cigarette, a Chesterfield King and start his usual dialogue:

"Everywhere I look, dairy farms disappearing, orchards gone and roads everywhere. Pretty soon this whole damn state will be paved. Be all roads and highways, you'll see. No farms anywhere at all."

Of course, Melvin was right to a point, but right outside Rocky Neck, Interstate 95 has always been a two lane highway, each way, well before the time he spoke. Except, when it was first built, one lane each way until sometime in the early Sixties. The interstate highway continues to be the same to this day, only two lanes each way, always slow and full of traffic.

You better say a prayer on a summer weekend if you're heading east on 95 heading for the Rhode Island beaches or Cape Cod. The "Cape" as we say. It's usually *bummpa* to *bummpa*! Really wicked traffic! And thank God, for us all, those old toll booths are gone! It was a whole ten cents to cross the Saybrook Bridge and the same for the Gold Star Memorial Bridge in New London.

Were those booths worth all of the clogged traffic they created? We all hated them, Melvin included. He ranted and raved about having to pay a toll all the time and for once, I agreed with him.

Melvin and I got along better after an incident happened to me in my second year at the park. It's in one of the following summer tales . . . do read on.

MELVIN'S OLD SIDEKICK, EDDIE

Melvin's buddy was Eddie, a carpenter who was going blind, but Melvin covered for him so he wouldn't lose his job. We all learned to do that.

He and Eddie would just go out and measure buildings in their spare time if they had nothing else to do.

Sometimes, if it was raining I'd go out with them, usually to the bathhouses. It didn't matter what measured reading I gave them, Melvin would just write it down on a paper with a pencil. He carried that pencil on his ear, under his hat and would always lick the tip of it before he wrote.

Eddie had a metal detector to find coins. Each morning he'd hit the beach and would bring back some loose change to our shop, where we all met every morning. We swore it was the same amount of coins every day. One day, a buddy of mine and I wanted to get back at cranky, ole Eddie.

We went and bought packs of BB's and threw them all over the beach before we left one evening. The next day Eddie came in shop, stomping and swearing a blue streak, "Some sons of bitches threw these damn BBs all over the beach. I didn't make a cent! Bastards!"

His hand was full of red copper BBs. Everyone gave a smile but said nothing. We all respected ole Eddie even though the word had gotten around that we had played a trick on him.

The same was true for most of the older workers at the park. All of us young guys paid them respect and rightfully so. Most were World War II or Korean vets.

"SPEAK LiTTLE, DO MUCH."

BENJAMiN FRANKLiN

"PENNIES ARE A START" AND MR. DEE

A long-time park veteran, old Mr. Dee and I worked together three of my four summers at the park. I always addressed him as Mr. Dee, because he treated me with respect when others didn't.

I also admired him for his resiliency in the face of adversity given the prejudice he'd faced in the 1940s and '50s. He talked about these things very rarely and when he did it was in hushed tones.

Short in stature and skinny, he always wore a small straw fedora on his head. He was a man of few words. When he was ready to say something, he'd take off his hat, rub his head, light a cigarette and speak. He didn't speak to too many people, but we hit it off right away and when we were alone sometimes he'd speak or answer my questions. I was lucky I guess, with him sharing his life with me.

Those times Mr. Dee did decide to speak, I'd sit down because I knew it was important to him and I didn't want to be distracted by anything.

He was an old school, black man from North Carolina and with his white peers, Mr. Dee mostly spoke only when spoken to. Down south, in the Tar Heel State, he had worked in a lumber mill and learned the hard way his place in society back then. He said he thought he'd be able to have a better life up north, so he moved with his family up north to Connecticut back in the fifties.

Mr. Dee told me in whispers about the abuse black men received back then if they spoke up too much or complained. He did neither. I really liked him and did whatever he told me to do.

We always gave each other a big grin when we saw each other and a handshake. I really liked and admired this man. He treated me as an equal and as an adult even though I was so young.

Mr. Dee never referred to me as "Stink," like the others did because of my first job at the park, but instead, he always called me "Slick." I liked being called Slick, much better than Stink.

Every day I looked forward to working with him. I tried to sign up to work with him every morning, before anyone else did.

Mr. Dee usually drove one of the big lawn mowers, a large tractor with twelve foot sliding blades on each side. As for me, I pushed the small lawn mower and ran around like a monkey, mowing all the areas he couldn't reach, especially the round posts that lined all of the paved roads to the entrance of the park.

If we were mowing and he saw a copper penny reflection, he'd stop his rig, turn off the tractor and point to what he saw. What is it, I thought? Geez, it was only a penny! We're stopping for that??

I'd grab it off the ground and hand it to him. He'd bow his head and smile in approval and slowly put the penny in his pocket like it was a piece of gold or an ancient ritual.

"Pennies are a start." he'd say.

Today, when I'm out walking anywhere and I see a penny on the ground, I always pick it up and say to myself, here you are, Mr. Dee, pennies are a start.

Mr. Dee, his straw hat and his smile still come right back in my mind. When I put the penny in my pocket, I bow my head like he would.

Like I said before, Mr. Dee usually only spoke when spoken to. If someone stopped by us in their car and asked us for directions or something, Mr. Dee would ask me to speak. If it was a white woman he froze, stopped and would point to me.

The first time he did this and pointed to me, I asked him why didn't he answer her and he told me this: "I'm from North Carolina and where I'm from ain't no black man gonna speak to no white woman and I'm not gonna start now." I looked a little bewildered and felt hurt for him at the same time. I shrugged my shoulders, "Well, ok, I guess" I replied. I told him he was in New England now and times were different. I was raised in the projects in New London and no one ever acted in that extreme prejudiced way that I came across.

"You ok, Mr. Dee?" I asked. He just nodded his head and started his tractor back up.

So, to honor Mr. Dee's wishes, I did all the talking if someone stopped us to ask a question and of course, gave him all of the pennies we found. He always worked hard and never complained about the heat, the humidity, the pay or having to get stuck working with me most summer days.

Now you know some of the reasons I now throw and try to find pennies at the park. To Mr. Dee, these pennies seemed magical. Finding one made his day and he would give me that rare smile.

I can still hear him softly say, "Pennies are a start."

THE SPY

At the park we had a spy who was also an assistant ranger, Mr. Kurry. His main job was to keep an eye on all of us workers – permanent or part-time and report back to Head Ranger Mr. Royal, on the work we were or weren't doing.

Melvin and Eddie hated Mr. Kurry and if they saw him from a distance they'd take their tools, hand braces for drilling holes, saws, hammers, whatever they had, and throw them down and just sit. They saw it as an insult!

Of course there were some people who were slackers but by and large everyone worked hard and carried their own weight. We mostly walked all day and carried whatever tools we needed, hauling garbage to be dumped and items to be fixed, on our backs.

Even though I was pretty young, by the time I ate dinner at home, I was exhausted and went to bed early. No beach parties for me back then.

Anyway, to get even with Mr. Kurry, someone took the four hub caps off his car, filled them with all kinds of fish and slapped them back on his vehicle! Needless to say, his car had all kinds of flies all over it, especially those nasty biting horse flies. He'd say, "My car stinks to high heaven but I have no idea where it's coming from!"

I never knew when or if Mr. Kurry found the culprit but it gave even my old lawn mowing buddy, Mr. Dee, a reason to smile and shake his head. Mr. Dee would watch Mr. Kurry check out the engine under his hood, looking for the reason for the smell, close it up and look bewildered. Mr. Dee would take off his hat, and rub his bald head to stifle a laugh.

Nobody I knew ever let on to Mr. Kurry and the poor guy's car stunk all summer.

ROCKY NECK STATE PARK – A SHORT HISTORY

Beach at Rocky Neck looking East 10/2022

Rocky Neck is that rather small half mile arc of beach where the masses of the glaciers dropped off their bundles of boulders and rocks the size of small Volkswagen Bugs into the sea. It's where in the 1930s, a break water was built to keep the swimmers safe from the currents and tides. The railroad, runs straight through the ocean facing side of the park and has been in use since 1848. It was the New Haven to New London Railroad line.

The large, wooden pavilion crowning the park, is a site to be seen and to walk through. It rises up from the beach like large curved stone crescent hotel where inside, each large weight bearing log comes from each area of Connecticut. Not only was the park developed in the 30s but the Ellie Mitchell Pavilion was completed in 1936. It is the largest Depression Era structure in the state!

Drive in and park in the upper parking lot and walk across the well-designed footbridge built in 1934. It was built before the great stone pavilion. I'm sure the bridge was completed in time to bring materials across to build the pavilion; tons and tons of rock and the huge wooden timbers that hold it all up. Quite a task, to put men back to work, completed during the Depression. I bet most of it was built by hand. Few or no machine tools of any kind back then. Extremely tedious and dangerous work.

I would have loved to talk to some of the builders, how much was the hourly wage, where did they live, who got hurt and how long did the building take to construct? These are but a few of the questions I'd ask. I guess when I worked there some of these men might have still been alive but I never thought of it. I was too young then to think about looking back.

Take some time to go inside this wooden encased arena. You'll see hand hewn picnic tables, huge supporting posts and lots of fireplaces. It's like a great medieval hall, where the Knights of the Round Table could have met perhaps someone from Connecticut in King Arthur's Court, I imagine.

Some said the park was developed to take the pressure off the other state park in Connecticut, Hammonasset, about 30 miles west of Rocky Neck.

Hopefully, sometime you'll take the time to walk, swim, hike and picnic at Rocky Neck.

Hammonasset Beach, looking towards Meigs Point 10/2022

HAMMONASSET – MY PLANTiNGS OF IVY AND ROSES

I also did some work at Connecticut's largest state beach, Hammonasset. I spend much of my current summertime there, as I own a nearby beach cottage. It is a beautiful park with three miles of beach front, a rocky breakwater, and three pavilions to choose from. We locals usually just call it "Hammo." It is the number one public attraction in Connecticut.

One summer, for a few weeks, they trucked us out there so we could transplant of all things, poison ivy to keep people off the dunes. We also planted Beach Roses which have sharp thorns and would also do the job. That was the reason they gave us for these plantings, to preserve the dunes and the beach front. I can still see the poison ivy and Beach Roses growing to this day from our back breaking handiwork and plantings.

We were on the way from Rocky Neck. It was hot, humid and stifling, sitting in the back of those trucks, on the metal beds with our tools in our hands and not much else. No water, food, shade or chairs. Maybe a Thermos of coffee if we were lucky!

Once they dropped us off at the entrance, we walked to different areas of the park, even to the end of the park, Meigs Point, about three miles away.

We carried our shovels, spades over our shoulders and lugged boxes of Beach Roses. There were no electric golf carts to truck us out there like the employees have today. Then again, like I said before, I can't remember anyone back then being overweight in the slightest way. Probably we were all thin from the constant walking and tedious work. We had no fast food chains back then either, and I never ate French fries or drank soda. Not that I didn't like those food items, they just weren't available to me or to the general public.

We got a whopping $2.25 an hour for transplanting poison ivy, and for planting the Beach Roses, instead of our usual $1.85. It was miserable work and some of us got covered with the poison ivy rash and most of us got cut up handling those super sharp thorny Beach Roses! We had ladies in this group who wanted to do this work to make the extra money and they suffered too. Most of them only lasted a few days of planting. It's not that they couldn't do the work, but the ladies didn't want the ivy rash or all the thorn cuts. But we kept them on our crew so they could make the big bucks. They helped us unload the trucks and somehow found water for us to drink.

Beautiful Beach Rose plants along the Niantic River, 9/2022

Speaking of the Beach Rose plants, they are not indigenous to the United States. They are considered an invasive species that spreads very easily, no thanks to us park workers from the sixties.

Beach Roses are from northeastern China, Japan, Korea and southeastern Siberia. There, they too are found on sand dunes.

The plants were introduced to the United States in the mid 1800s as an ornamental plant. Each edible part, like the rose bud, can also be used to make an excellent warming brew.

We did other work at Hammo too, like fixing up the old wooden boardwalks, which rotted away almost every year. Now, everyone at the parks uses composite plastic wood for building boardwalks, and stainless steel screws and they don't ever rot or rarely need replacement. These new composite boards and stainless steel screws are great as they require little or no maintenance.

Those old boardwalks would split, splinter and beachgoers were constantly getting sharp wood slivers in their feet, especially kids. Also people would get stuck and cut on all those rusty exposed nails. A tetanus shot waiting to happen!

Two of the workers, who were part of the Hammonasett crew and not Rocky Neck, were supposed to be helping us with the plantings. Every day, they'd disappear and I wouldn't see them until the end of the day. They would head out to Meigs Point and then come back giggling. I didn't want to know what they were doing and I didn't care but they were of no use to the rest of us and were getting that extra pay for doing nothing. I was angry with them, thinking they had pulled a fast one on the rest of us.

The guy was David along with his girlfriend Maureen. He thought he was a big shot and tried to impersonate

President Kennedy by always saying things like, "Do it with *viga!*" He did nothing with vigor or *viga*. David's hands were always clean and white. No work was ever done from that kid and Maureen was infatuated with him because he drove an Opel sports car. To me that car was ugly. It looked like a small mouse. Maureen did even less work and complained more than David did, if that was at all possible.

After two days of this crap, I told Melvin back at Rocky Neck to try to remove the two from the work detail. I said they were worthless and everyone was ticked off at them. He said "Ok Rich, no problem."

The next morning, just after arriving at Hammonasett, David came up to me while we were unloading more Beach Rose plants and tools off the trucks. "Rich, you bastard, I heard you took Maureen and me off our $2.25 an hour job."

"Yeah," I said, "You both didn't want to work, so you got your wish. Eat my shorts and get the hell out of here!" Nobody said the "F" word back then. All the other workers laughed at him, some also told him to get lost and he left in disgrace. I thought for a moment I might have to get in a fight with David but I didn't want to lose my job. I needed the money for college. Thanks to my crew for backing me up, no fight was needed. Not trusting him, I kept an eye on him whenever he was around. I didn't want to get sucker punched or worse.

Everyone was happy those two malingerers were gone and I heard they both got fired not long after that. Good riddance to them and another good life lesson learned: be fair and honest to everyone you work with, work as hard as everyone else does and they will support you in return. If you have people who don't do their part, get rid of them. No excuses accepted.

I guess I had an itch to make extra money that summer. Go visit Hammonasett State Park and view the poison ivy and Beach Rose plants. Just don't touch either one unless you're wearing gloves.

Beautiful poison ivy! 9/2022

About poison ivy, we all grew up with that adage, "leaves of three let it be." It can be pretty and colorful sometimes, red in the spring, shiny green in the summer and orange, yellow, or red in the fall. But even in the winter, with no leaves on it, it can still be dangerous if you happen to touch the roots.

Along with poison ivy, Connecticut has poison oak and poison sumac, two other variations. Some people try to pick it up and smell it, thinking it's the more fragrant sumac plant. It's not – so I repeat, "Leaves of three, let it be."

MY DAD'S SUMMER MEMORY

My father said that during his summers off from school in New London, he, his sister and my grandparents, would take the trolley at least once a year, out to the Rocky Neck beach probably in the early thirties. He said that the men and women covered up pretty discretely back then and had extra clothes they took on the trolley. He said the trip to Rocky Neck was an all-day affair.

My dad, unlike my mom wasn't much of a beach person but even Rocky Neck stirred memories in him from his childhood. On the weekends he really didn't want to go to the beach, but if we suggested Rocky Neck, he usually said ok and always seemed enjoy himself. He'd come home with a salt water itchy body and a nice beach sunburn to complain about the next day.

Rocky Neck, when I started working there, was as familiar as putting on an old shoe. I had been there many times with my parents, grandparents, aunt and my uncle. My cousins, Lauren, Christine, Cynthia, my sister Paula, my brother Michael and I would pick bombulines, an Italian word for sea snails or periwinkles, as they are sometimes called.

My grandmother would let them soak for a day or so in her basement. She kept rinsing them in water and then cooked them up in a homemade tomato sauce with some anise flavorings. It was a very tasty treat, indeed.

There's a small membrane door on the end of the shell. You first remove it to get at the body of the sea snail. Then you use the end of a safety pin to pick the snail up and eat it. Not much to look at, but they taste much better than I can ever describe it! Yum!

When I go visit Rocky Neck, I can never find these sea snails anymore. We must have picked them clean. I hope not, maybe it was just high tide.

Crowded beach scene, Rocky Neck, 8/2022

MR. ROYAL

Mr. Royal ruled the park at Rocky Neck as well he should have, as he was the park's first park ranger. He had been there since the thirties when the park was created. Ranger Royal was strict, demanding, honest, fair, and had all of our respect. He always wore his Smokey Bear style hat and under his tenure the park was in great shape. He had a slight limp but that didn't slow him down. He was all over the park. You never knew when he was going show up, view what everyone was doing and freely giving his opinion.

Rocky Neck was his domain and he wanted people, cars and workers to respect his park. No dogs allowed, no floatation devices in the water, no alcohol allowed in his park.

He'd say, "Park the cars tight and narrow, get them to pull in quickly. We'll have a full park today, about 50,000 people!"

Beachgoers were to unload at the designated area, pack everything for the day into a provided large wheeled cart then bring it back for the next person to use. If you tried to park in the unloading zone, you'd get a ticket faster than you could sneeze.

I remember telling a guy not to park in the loading zone. He said, "I no speak the English" I told him if he parks there he'll get a ticket and his car would be towed. He quickly said, "Oh, ok, I move!!"

Once in a while I helped out at one of the gates. It was $1 admission during the week, $2 on the weekend. Such a deal! But even then, some people couldn't afford it so I'd just wave them through.

A woman with a station wagon full of kids, would say, "$2??? You have to be kidding? I only have $1!" I waved her through. Seniors, military vets, people in old clunker cars, I'd wave them all through, no charge for admission.

It was like they'd won the Irish Sweepstakes, when I waved them through. I was always down on ticket sales. I said I went to the bathroom a lot or fewer people drove up to my booth. But I made a lot of beachgoers happy.

Word must have gotten around, because if I worked a front gate on a given weekend, I was very busy. A lot of cars veered over to my booth! I don't believe Mr. Royal ever found out why my weekend ticket sales were so low.

Every Monday we started to clean up the park and it took us all five days until Friday to get ready for the next weekend. Garbage runs and more garbage runs and fighting the seagulls to keep it clean. Raking the sand, mowing all the lawns and picking up the endless litter. The gulls had learned long ago to tip the cans over and scavenge with their beaks creating a huge mess with each garbage can. But back to Mr. Royal.

Once, Chief Ranger Royal had the bright idea to line the bottom of the garbage cans with cement to prevent the gulls from doing their dirty work but then lifting them up to empty them was tough!

I'm short and had to lift these cement garbage cans up over my head. Sometimes my hand would get impaled on the side of the truck with my hand stuck in the heavy garbage can. The truck would take off and I'd get dragged along screaming or else I'd get a "*drippa*" down my arm and face from some week old food or stale contraband beer. That made everyone, especially the hated lifeguards, laugh.

Mr. Royal seemed to appreciate the work we maintenance crews did. When he drove by, he'd stop and say, "Good job boys." He never mentioned the lifeguards to any of us but I got the feeling that he saw them as an unwanted necessity. To him, we did all the work to keep his park the way he wanted it to look and we were essential. The lifeguards really didn't do much except on weekends, when they had huge crowds to watch.

Maintenance guys couldn't stand the lifeguards, those prissy, rich boys who never had to clean, repair anything or make garbage runs. The only exercise they got was running on the beach, sitting in a guard stand, waving their pith helmets and blowing their whistles.

Needless to say, the lifeguards and my maintenance buddies were not on friendly terms.

No girl lifeguards were to be had back then. All the girls worked in the bath change houses cleaning or manning a first aid station. The first aid station could be pretty busy, especially on the weekends. Adults and kids were always getting splinters in the bottoms of their feet from the old wooden boardwalks. They'd get jelly fish stings or the worst thing to happen was when sometimes young kids went barefoot.

People having a cookout would sometimes just dump their used coals anywhere, instead of leaving them in the fire pit. If Mr. Royal caught people dumping their cook out charcoals illegally or if we reported it, he'd quickly give them a park summons.

Just tossing out these hot coals was not only dangerous but it also caused small brush fires.

Adults, but mostly kids would step on these coals barefoot and come screaming into the aid stations with severely burned feet. The girls on duty would do what they could and quickly called an ambulance. I would see this happen about four or five times each summer. The first aid station personnel, mostly young girls in training to be nurses, did what they could to calm people down with varied beach injuries.

Other girls worked in the concession stands. They'd be slinging snow cones, cooking up hamburgs, French fries and splitting hot dogs at a rapid pace. I could never afford those beach prices and packed my food in a metal lunch box.

Twenty-five cents for a snow cone you say?? What a rip off! But then again, you were at the beach! I quickly learned to flirt with the girls at the concession stands to get free food to come my way or a free pack of cigarettes for "Bullet Bob," one of the permanently hired guys.

Once in a while when I got a free hotdog, I always told the girls, "I'd like my buns toasted," which made them all laugh. It was hot in those concession stands and no one had air conditioning, maybe a fan if you were lucky.

One thing I do remember about Chief Ranger Royal was that he taught me to respect everything about Rocky Neck and to treat it like it was my own. This is a feeling I still have to this day for Rocky Neck and all the other state parks.

Mr. Royal and I had one bone of contention, but that's in the next chapter. He was doing his job, I was at fault and it was a lesson learned that has helped me to this day. Read on, as I don't want to give it away.

> "LIFE IS SHORT. BREAK THE RULES."
>
> MARK TWAIN

WEDNESDAY OFF AND JANICE

There was a girl, Janice Zapp, not her real last name, but close enough, whom I met the first year I worked at the park. I was smitten with her from the start.

She was the prettiest thing I had ever seen. She was Italian like me, a real spaghetti bender. Janice's eyes were like black olives, and hair was as dark as midnight and she had a wonderful grin. She was very smart and loved to laugh. When I said something stupid to get her attention, she'd put her hand on her chin and just smile and shake her head.

I was attracted to her so much, my head would spin when she spoke and I couldn't concentrate on a word she'd say. Whenever I laid my peepers on her, it was like a two by four had just hit me on the noggin. I was just another numb, dumb teenager.

She was from Hartford and her parents camped in a yellow and white camper for the summer, at Rocky Neck. Her parents drove a light green Ford, a small model. Or it was maybe a Dodge Dart? I looked for that car every day to see if she was in it.

Janice worked at the Eastern Bath House by the first aid station helping the nurse and then cleaning up the ladies change room.

I'd make sure I had that area of the beach to clean so I could go down and flirt with her. While there one day, I finally got the nerve to ask her out. We were going to go to Rhode Island, to one of the fantastic beaches there, Misquamicut.

Sometimes on the weekends she'd work the main gate, handing out tickets and taking money from those who drove through and didn't have a camping pass. I would always tell Mr. Dee I had to mow by the park entrance on the weekends when Janice worked one of the main gates. He'd just shake his head, smile and nod okay. He knew why I wanted to work down there and I always took my time mowing! When it came to Janice, I could be a professional at wasting time.

I had a light blue, 1965, MGB convertible, a real chick magnet, I thought. Nice looking car but mechanically a mess. That car was always breaking down. It had carburetor problems, engine gas pump stalling and constant electrical issues.

Once, I took Janice on a trip to New York City to see the sights. In Manhattan, we went over a sharp bump and it shook up one of the battery cables. The car had two six volt batteries, each one just as expensive as a one twelve volt. It shorted every light out in the car! My headlights, radio lights and more importantly the instrument panel, all went black. I eventually had to replace all of them. What fun that was. So, I was stuck in New York City with no lights working on my car.

I went into a local hardware store and bought two flashlights. After buying four D cell batteries, I turned them on, EB Greened

(another chapter) them to the front of the MGB and headed for home down Interstate 95.

Janice was astounded, but I told her we had no other choice. She said, "Wow, I'll never forget this trip or this car!"

We received constant laughs at every toll booth. One guy said, "And I thought I'd seen everything! Good luck getting home, kids. No toll charge for you guys tonight." Well, we made it, thanks to well lit highways. Another fun and dangerous trip in that money pit! I got Janice safely back to Rocky Neck, mostly by following the cars in front of me. We never told her parents what had happened.

Once, I got so mad at the MGB, I kicked it and put a big dent in the side. Well, that didn't fix whatever the problem was and I in turn, received a nice sore foot. It was always much more of a mechanic's magnet than a chick magnet.

More than once, Janice had to push the car backwards to release the starter Bendix, then run and push it forward so I could release the clutch. I saved some gas with that car and she got a workout.

I asked her what day she had off, since at the park, we only had off one day a week. Her day off was Wednesday. I asked her to go to Misquamicut, that great state beach in Rhode Island known for the large waves, cleaner ocean water than you could find in Long Island Sound and great for body surfing. From that day on, my day off was also to be Wednesday!

That's when the park job tried to get in the way of my chance to have a date with Janice. But I just couldn't, wouldn't, shouldn't let that happen.

The following Monday morning, before the crew set out with our jobs to be completed for the day, Al told us what day we were to do extra jobs at the park. The one we all dreaded was the seven outhouses right outside the park known as the "Magnificent Seven."

The Magnificent Seven name came from the popular movie back in 1960. It starred Yul Brynner, Charles Bronson and a young Steve McQueen, among others. Everyone had seen it either at the movies, (I saw it at the old Garde Movie Theater when we lived in New London) or on a black and white TV. It was very enjoyable but that's as far as the coincidence went.

Yes, there were seven outhouses but they were far from magnificent. They were always gross, with human feces, dirty clothes, condoms, women's feminine napkins smeared all over and other items you couldn't even imagine, much less have to smell. I once put one of my long gloves on and fished out a guy's glass eye for ten dollars! I never asked how it wound up in there.

Sometimes to christen a new worker, once they got in the outhouse, we'd sneak up on the outside and tip it over so the door was on the downside and they were stuck inside! We never heard so much yelling and screaming, even to this day. It was funny, as long as it didn't happen to you!

So Al says, "Valentini, Wednesday, is your day for cleaning the Magnificent Seven." I thought, damn, that's the day I need to take off, to go cruising with Janice to Misquamicut in my hot 65 MGB convertible.

Rich cleaning an outhouse. Rocky Neck, summer of 1968.

After he went around assigning these extra jobs to all the other summer help for the week, Al then asked me what day during the week I wanted to have off.

Of course I said, "Wednesday." Nobody caught it except for Mr. Dee, who smiled ear to ear. "Oh, Slick," he said, "You gonna get it now."

So I picked up Janice that Wednesday morning and we headed to Misquamicut in Rhode Island. I never mentioned to her about the Magnificent

Seven fiasco! But as the week went on, of course she found out.

The weather was great but we hit all of the backed-up traffic after we turned off of 95. Going through Pawcatuck and crossing the river into Westerly took forever, and I tried to avoid all of the bumper kisses. But, we passed the time listening and singing to the top ten new hits on the radio. Especially, "Cracklin' Rosie" by Neil Diamond. I'd wave my hands in her face when I sang and do other annoying things and that made the time go by until we got to the beach.

Janice looked great. She had on a pink and white bikini and was sitting on a blanket next to me. What a lucky guy I was! We ate some pizza that tasted like cardboard with tomato sauce and got some fried clams. Who cared about food? I had that one day with her all to myself.

We went swimming in the rollers, laughing and splashing each other like two little kids. In the water, I dunked her a couple of times. On the last dunk, she came up gasping for air and told me to stop and help her out of the water. I had always dunked my brother, Michael and he had no problems with it. But with Janice, it was different! She got scared and then I felt ashamed.

I carried her to the blanket and promised her I wouldn't do that again. She sputtered out a "Thanks," and still feeling guilty, I went and got her something to drink.

When I returned to our blanket, I kissed her, rolled myself and my beach towel up to her and kissed her again! We went back in the ocean and I let her dunk me. She was laughing in revenge as she held my head under the water.

With the sun and the wind coming off the beach, we both started to look like red lobsters and would suffer that night and at work the next day.

Doing physical work and having to do it with a sunburn would be painful! So, before we knew it, we had to go to the bathhouses to change, shower and drive back before all the Electric Boat traffic got out in Groton.

Thirty thousand people worked at Electric Boat, now called General Dynamics, building submarines. My grandfather and dad both had worked there. The employees got out at staggered times but I didn't want to get stuck in traffic again or have her back late on our first date.

We hit some EB traffic but not too badly. Pretty soon there was exit 72 off of I-95 to Rocky Neck.

Traveling around that quick turn of an exit, I again hit more traffic! What was the problem?

Oh no, there was line of people waiting to get into the park, even during the week! I thought I'm not sitting in line again and I know everyone at the front gate, so why not show Janice my expert driving skills and just drive over the dunes, get back on the road and avoid the gate. I thought, they know it's me in my MGB. I'll be ok. I gunned the engine and turned off the road. Zippity-zip, I'll just drive over the dunes at the quick.

Janice and I hit the sand dune and flew into the air like John Glenn in a rocket off Cape Canaveral. I didn't realize how high the dune was. The car bottomed out and both of our heads jerked forward and the jolt snapped our necks back. Then the MGB spun around like the spin cycle on a washing machine.

Janice said, "Oh my God!" but at least we made it and weren't hurt. "Sorry" I told her. I was glad only one gatekeeper saw me do that stupid move, but as luck would have it, the head ranger, Mr. Royal was in the booth that day and saw whole thing. I was dead meat but didn't know it at the time.

We drove up to Janice's folks' trailer and I kissed her quickly so her parents or fellow campers wouldn't stare. They all did anyway.

"Janice, I loved spending the day with you." "See you tomorrow at work and can we do this again next Wednesday?"

Janice replied, "I'm sure it will be fine. I'd like to go again next Wednesday. Rich, try to drive down and visit me at the East Pavilion tomorrow if you can, OK?" Yes, I thought. Tomorrow, East Pavilion, I'm on it. I'll figure out how to get there. And next Wednesday's day off couldn't come fast enough.

The next day though . . . . I caught hell.

When I walked into our early morning assignment area, where we all met each day, everyone broke into cheers and started clapping, even old Mr. Dee. "What did I do?" I asked. Melvin proudly said, "Rich, you took yesterday off. Everyone else at the park was really busy and so the lifeguards were sent outside of the park and had to clean up the Magnificent Seven. We all loved it."

That was the first time Melvin called me by my name Rich, instead of Stink. After that, no one ever called me Stink again. I was their hero. You see, the lifeguards, were the pompous, royalty of the park and were treated with kid gloves. Why? I had no idea? I always supposed because they were rich and admired by the park employers in some way. Or maybe in their way of thinking, people who used their hands to work, were somehow beneath them. I guess this same foolish idea still holds true in the minds of some people even today.

The lifeguards never had to pick anything up, empty garbage cans, clean anything or do any menial work. We summer maintenance workers were the bottom feeders. They thought they were the cocks of the walk. That they had to clean up those seven gross port-a-potties made me laugh too, but not for long because just then, our main boss of Rocky Neck, Chief Ranger Mr. Royal, drove up.

He stepped out of his car and hobbled up to me. "God damn it, Valentini! You had this park in an uproar yesterday. You knew you had the job to maintain those toilets outside the park on Wednesday and yet you took the day off."

"Al gave me the day off when I asked him." I replied.

"Your job comes first and I saw you yesterday as well, avoid the ticket booth and drive over the dune almost killing yourself and whoever was in the car."

"Yes," I said. "That was pretty stupid Mr. Royal, I won't do that again. I apologize."

"Yes, the hell you won't! You ever do a stunt like that again and you're fired!" I silently nodded my head in agreement.

"Today, you will clean those outhouses at the end of the day and every Sunday afternoon when the park clears out, that will be one of your jobs as well."

"Ok," I replied. And I thought, well, at least I can keep having Wednesday off and spend those days with Janice. I didn't care. I was happy with the outcome and everyone silently smiled at me and when Mr. Royal wasn't looking, they all gave me a thumbs up.

Old Mr. Dee said to me after everyone had dispersed, "Oh, Slick, I'm just glad you weren't fired." "Thanks, I told him, "I would have missed you too. I should have listened to you last week."

But unbeknownst to me, the war was on with the lifeguards.

A MiD-SUMMERS DAYDREAM

Of the trips in life I won't forget,
Were the summers taking Janice to Misquamicut,
That snail slow drive through Pawcatuck
    and Westerly,
Every Wednesday we'd go with glee!

R. Valentini

THE LiFEGUARD WAR

The lifeguards were pissed that they had to clean up those outhouses and felt that I had humiliated all of them. Oh my, the guards, our uncrowned kings of the park. They had to join the ranks of us downtrodden for part of one day and do some of our work. Those poor slobs.

They had heard through the grapevine that the job was supposed to be mine that day and I had taken the day off to avoid doing it. Nothing could be further from the truth! I really didn't like cleaning those filthy, nasty things; nobody did, but I always did what I was assigned. It was my job, no complaints. I didn't think I had options. And as I learned from Mr. Royal, you did what you were assigned. I just wanted to do it on any day other than Wednesday.

It was really all Janice's fault, (just kidding), but no one knew why I wanted that day off except Mr. Dee. Ha!

To get back at me, the lifeguards found out where I had to work on most days and on my garbage dumping days, they put rocks about a quarter way up inside the garbage cans so I couldn't lift them up to empty them. I'd fall down on the ground covered in garbage or else have my hand stuck on the inner side of the truck, screaming in pain! My hand and wrist still hurt thinking about it. At the end of the day, my hands were a bloody, bruised mess.

After about the third day of this misery, one of the newer hired guys had just returned from Vietnam. He was always throwing a big Bowie knife around and acting bizarre. I'm sure he was having flashbacks from the war and he had anger issues to boot. Sometimes his violent behavior scared me. He threw that stupid knife everywhere. I thought that someday, that knife would ricochet off something and land in my leg.

The next morning, this Vietnam vet drove us up to the house where the lifeguards could stay if they wanted. It was a nice little old house and the guards could stay there all summer instead of driving back and forth to work all the time. We maintenance guys weren't provided that option.

The lifeguards were just starting to come outside, milling around laughing about something. All of a sudden, we pulled up with the brakes squeaking, leaves and dust flying.

Our crazy driver, gets out of the cab, whips out his Bowie knife and throws it at the front door the guards had just left from! It stuck in with a twang sound just like in the movies. Thank God he didn't hit anyone or no one else came out at that exact time.

"Hey assholes!" he yelled, "Anyone ever again puts rocks in the garbage cans or messes with Rich; the next time, I won't miss!!" I hoped he was just kidding but didn't want to ask. He shouted out a few more choice expletives and with that we left. I felt as if I had just been vindicated.

With that, my one week of war with the guards was over and of course, they never had to clean up the Magnificent Seven again. But, I did. I never spoke to the lifeguards when I saw them and they all left me alone and were silent. It was a truce that held all that summer long.

And then again, best of all, I still had Wednesdays off to be with Janice. Yes.

> "USE IT UP, WEAR IT OUT,
> MAKE IT DO OR DO WITHOUT."
>
> AN OLD YANKEE DEPRESSION ERA PROVERB.

EB GREEN IT

"EB green it." That's what everyone told us at Rocky Neck when we had to repair something. EB green was a super strong type of green colored duct tape. My brother-in-law Roger, who was a sonar man on an U.S. Navy attack submarine always carried a roll in his car.

I'm sure it was used to connect heating and cooling ducts on the submarines, thus the name duct, not "duck tape," as some misinformed people say today.

It wasn't the type you'd be able to buy in the store. My dad would bring rolls of it home from Electric Boat or EB. I asked him once how he got it home and he said in his lunch pail. My grandad, who also worked at EB also had rolls of the tape that could adhere to anything. He too, brought them home in his metal lunch pail. I suppose everyone did that back then.

In my grandad's basement were lots of brand new tools; pliers, wrenches, and screwdrivers. He didn't drive a car and couldn't go shopping at Sears on weekends. That's where most people bought all of their tools back then.

I asked my grandfather where all the tools had come from. He said in broken English, "The crazy Navy. Every time the submarine come to dry dock for refit, they replace all tools with new ones. I pick them out of the garbage when no one looking. Crazy Navy, no?"

This EB green was also very handy growing up in Connecticut. I remember all of the stores were closed on Sundays. The only places you go were the local gas stations where you could buy gasoline for your car, milk and bread and that's it. No Chiclets (little squares of gum in a small flat box), not one stinking Sugar Daddy, no pack of five cent State Line potato chips but the worst of all for me, no baseball cards. Those were my four favorite items. How dreadful! I just loved those old Connecticut Blue Laws. Not.

Actually, the Blue Laws were rather nice in that families spent the day together, because very few people worked on Sundays. It was the one day a week I saw my dad, as he usually worked six days a week at Electric Boat. His only fun hobby was playing his clarinet and saxophone at Lamperelli's Bar on Bank Street in New London or playing a dance job with Dick Campo's Band. My Dad loved to play the Big Band sound. But back to EB green, our weekend savior.

So, if you needed a home repair of a busted water pipe, a broken window, a wiring problem and you tried to fix it, you used... you guessed it ... EB green. Just "EB green it." as everyone said.

Broken arm's sling, impromptu dog muzzle, pin your brother's ears back so he wouldn't look like Dumbo or patch a hole in your bedroom wall – for everything, you used that handy Yankee cure-all, EB green. Every handyman's and homeowner's secret weapon.

EB green had to hold everything together until Monday as you couldn't get any sort of repair parts because no stores were open on Sundays which is hard to conceive of today. Presently, we have mass marketing everywhere you look, with Amazon's next day service, and very few stores ever closing except for a few holidays. It truly was a different world, but not in a bad way. You learned to be patient and knew you had to wait.

If you want to fix it neat and clean, make sure you use that EB green.

So how does EB green tie in again with Rocky Neck? Well, Janice and I had a date one evening, around the fourth of July.

I told her I wanted to take her to see the fireworks over at Sound View in Old Lyme. It's a quaint little beach town.

Now you have to remember, compared to the rest of Eastern Connecticut, all of us were bottom feeders compared to Old Lyme. People who mentioned they were from Old Lyme seemed to drip with money. They could be pretty snooty as well. Guys wore their shirt collars up, and looked down with disdain on pretty much everyone else.

So we drove over. Janice looked and smelled great. I loved to put my nose in her hair and inhale. Ahhhhh. Janice would just laugh and push me away. "You poor boy!" she'd say. I parked the MGB down near the beach as close as I could get and we walked quite a way in the setting sun. The beach there was crowded and at Sound View all of the shops were open and they had items to purchase on sidewalk stands. I held her hand so I wouldn't lose her in the crowds. I had the MGB's convertible top up because the weather man on the radio said that later that night we might have a chance for a shower.

The town had a great fireworks show at Sound View. I bought ice cream cones for us and we watched the explosions, heard the booms and I repeatedly kissed her in between all of that noise. How could this evening get any better? It didn't. It quickly changed for the worst.

Returning to the car, I saw that someone had ripped a huge hole into the convertible top and poured some beer through the rip. I thought this tear will cost me a fortune. How much would it be for a new convertible top? I was afraid to contemplate it.

I had an old beach towel in the car and I used it to dry up the beer mess on our seats. I always had such awful luck with that car.

Then it started to shower. But what did I have to fix the hole and to stop the rain from coming inside the car?

Yes, you guessed it. A roll of EB green to the rescue. We quickly taped up the rip and it held with no water in the cab. Thank you EB green. It saved the day again or in that case the night.

I don't know if they make it anymore or if the Navy still uses EB green duct tape. I haven't seen it in some thirty odd years, but if they do make it, find it and keep it.

Now you know about not only finding the magical pennies but also that magical duct tape, EB green.

Just EB green it.

THE BRUSH STROKE

Fat Freddie nervously chomped on his ubiquitous "guinea *stinka*" cigar stuck in the corner of his mouth. He was huffing and puffing and breaking out into a nervous sweat. Taking off his pith helmet, he was shouting into his walkie talkie, his "bitch box."

"Tell everyone to get to the campground entrance. We have a brush fire that's growing fast!! Bring the fire engine up, too!"

Melvin got a call in our maintenance room near the entrance to the park. Most of us were up there on our coffee break.

"Ok, you guys." Melvin said. "Rich, Bob, Eddie, Tom, go get those Indian tanks, fill them with water and I'll show you how to use them! Make it quick, we have a brush fire in the campground."

For those of you who don't know, an Indian tank is a rather large metal tank of water that is strapped on your back with a pump and nozzle attached to it.

You pump the hose nozzle up and down and you can spray water about 100 feet or more.

Melvin shouted, "I'll get the old fire engine started up and take off ASAP. Fat Freddie will have a stroke over this brush fire and call out the National Guard if we don't hurry and get there!"

"So, Melvin, does that mean Fat Freddie could have a brush stroke?" I said with a grin.

'That's it exactly," Melvin replied "He'll have his tidy whiteys in a bind."

We all filled up our Indian tanks and started to pump them so they had enough pressure when we arrived on the scene. I thought old Eddie would fall over, the tank was so heavy. We looked like a bunch of shiny backed Japanese beetles.

Arriving at the scene, it was mass confusion. Smoke and people shouting orders was all I could see and hear. Then our fire engine arrived blaring its siren. It had an old crank siren that someone was stirring around like his hair was on fire.

Through the haze, I could see Fat Freddie, Ranger Royal, and Phil, the head of the campground, were all talking at the same time. Freddie was asking Mr. Royal if he should bring over the Niantic Fire Department of which he was the head.

"Oh no," Mr. Royal said, "We should be able to handle this. We don't need any more noise and confusion than we already have. The campers are already nervous and starting to leave. It's only a brush fire."

Then the fire engine pulled up. We all ran over and took hold of the hose and ran it towards the direction of the fire. Holding it up, thinking we had to hold it tight Melvin gave a thumbs up, that he was turning the water tank on.

Nothing came out. The hose was still limp in our hands. No one had ever checked to see if the fire engine's tank was filled with any water. We all started to laugh. Ranger Royal was not at all happy.

"Get that damn thing back up there and go put water in it!" he shouted. Ranger Royal threw up his hands and turned around saying, "Damn it, put this fire out!"

Fat Freddie belted out at us, "Bring up those Indian tanks and get to work! Spray the whole area."

As I started to spray water from my tank, I realized I was getting wet. The guys on the other side were spraying so high, they were hitting all of us. So then, we retaliated by doing the same to them. But, not old Eddie who fell over trying to put his tank on. He looked like a chrome turtle. Everyone got wet, Fat Freddie, Ranger Royal, and Phil and the brush fire was spreading. As it burned towards the road, the fire had nowhere to go and it started to die out, but not because we had done anything to stop it.

I actually started to wet down the burning embers at the same time I was spraying all the other park employees. Remember, I was only eighteen and thought that this was just another fun park employee experience. A huge squirt gun war and my side won.

We were all soaking wet, blackened from the smoke and smelling like an old charred hot dog. Melvin finally arrived back, with that useless fire engine again roaring its siren, but by then he could see that the fire was almost out.

Grabbing the hose, we doused what little was left burning and then that was it. All of this yelling and screaming like it was World War III was over in about thirty minutes. Out like a marshmallow puff.

I couldn't wait for another brush fire to happen that year and was disappointed that we never did have another one. What a blast with all the smoke, noise and confusion! I was a fire experienced summer employee.

Now that old fire engine was at the ready and old Eddie had learned how to put on an Indian tank without falling over.

That was my first brush with a fire. It was a brush fire that had almost caused Fat Freddie to get what I called a brush stroke.

THE LOST *COUGA* CAPER

Tommy was this young man at the park, probably mid-twenties, who wanted eventually to be a park ranger. He was living in his own trailer at the campground there at Rocky Neck.

Tall and skinny, he wore his pith helmet high up on his head, like it was in a shell. He wore large teardrop sunglasses that he had on rain or shine and talked fast with a strong New England accent.

His hero, like for most of us was our former president, John F. Kennedy, a fellow New Englander. Tommy said he liked JFK mostly, because as he said, "We finally had a president who had no accent."

Tommy had a whistle permanently hanging around his neck which he loved to blow at people and cars, for whatever reason.

His pride and joy was his light blue '68 Mercury Cougar and he talked about it constantly. "Hey, ya wanna see my new *cah*? A *Couga,* it's goor-gee-ous, huh?" Tommy would ask.

One morning, when we arrived and had been sitting in our shop waiting for Al to tell us what jobs we had to do for that day, a outburst occurred. Suddenly, Tommy came inside the room, yelling like a crazy man. He had a small cut on his forehead, with dried blood on his face and shirt.

"My *cah*, my *cah*" he shouted in his best accent, "I can't find my *cah*. You guys have to help me!"

Melvin looked at me and said, "Who the hell is that?"

"Oh, it's that young, ranger in training guy," I said. "His name is Tommy and he has a summer trailer here that he stays in at the campground. You've probably seen him drive around in that state car."

"Christ Almighty, kid, what's your problem?" Melvin asked.

Tommy shouted in dismay, "I lost my *Couga*, my beautiful *Couga* is missing!"

Oh my God, I thought. How could he be missing his car?

"Yeah, I got blitzed last night, and somehow I got back to the park. I think I wrecked my *cah*. I really don't remember. My *Couga* is somewhere. Can you guys please help me find it!" Tommy was desperate. "I have to get it before Mr. Royal finds out what I did or my ass is grass." He said he had crawled back to the campground and passed out near his trailer, woke up and couldn't remember what had happened or where his Cougar was.

Mr. Dee shook his headed and whispered to me, "That boy drinks too much and will kill somebody someday. I hope he'll never be a park ranger here."

I told Melvin that we should get two of our trucks and go find his car while it was still early. It shouldn't be that hard to find I hoped. Tommy looked at me and I said, "Tommy get in, let's go find your wonderful Mercury *Couga*."

Melvin and Mr. Dee got in one truck and went on one side of the park and Tommy, Eddie and I drove in our truck on the eastern side. In about ten minutes, after Tommy told me where he thought he had left it, we soon found the missing Cougar.

"My *Couga*, my *Couga*!" he shouted. "Oh, no!"

There it was, in the woods, stuck between two trees with the lights still on. What a mess. That poor car. Mr. Dee was right, it's lucky he didn't kill anyone that night.

The two front doors were crushed in and there was blood on one the seats headrest so that's how I figured he got out. He crawled over the front seat and went out the back door. I shook my head in disbelief. I wanted to laugh but couldn't.

Melvin and Mr. Dee showed up in their truck. We hitched up a chain and hooked to the rear of the Cougar while Tommy, Eddie and I pushed it from the rear. With a big creaking sound, we freed it.

That poor Cougar was totaled. As Tommy wailed about his poor car, Melvin told him to shut up and to thank God he was lucky to be still alive.

"Quit your drinking, kid." Melvin said. "You're just a smart ass punk and can't handle it. This is the last time you come to us when you screw up again. You got it?"

"Thank you, guys." Then he turned again, looking at his car, "Oh, my *cah*, my *Couga*, my *Couga*," lamented Tommy.

Tommy got into the front seat by crawling through the back seat and was able to drive that once beautiful car away. No one ever mentioned what happened with Tommy to Mr. Royal.

If we ever needed Tommy's help to clear traffic out of the way for our trucks, or help us on the park roads, he was always happy to oblige. He went out of his way to be of our assistance.

Every time we maintenance people drove by Tommy in our old, beat-up trucks, he would make a point of waving to us with his pith helmet. He wasn't your normal snobby young ranger, just sitting in a new, state Ford sedan, ignoring us.

It was like he was one of us and we appreciated that. He was happy we solved the case of his missing Cougar, or *Couga* as Tommy would have said. Plus, he kept the job that he loved and was able to buy his new love: a '69 light blue Mercury Cougar. Excuse me, I mean a new *Couga*! The Cougar Caper was over.

I never heard about him being drunk at Rocky Neck again. Hopefully he learned his life saving lesson.

YANKEE *WiSE CRACKiN'* AND A *YACKiN'*

Love the old New England accent – use your *blinka!*
That some say is fast *disappearin'*,
From Boston to New London – that *wicked stinka!*
The voices from my past, I find so *endearin'*.
Like that old *cab* – he bought a *clunka!*
As long as I'm alive, words I will *neva* tire a *hearin'*.

R. Valentini

HAY, A BUNDLE OF PROBLEMS?

In mid-summer or close to the beginning of fall, we started haying. For those of you who don't what this is, we'd cut all the tall grasses in the park. Mr. Dee and I mostly. Then we'd let it dry.

We'd drive a hay bailer to the site and bail the hay up in bundles for the deer and other animals to feed on or nest in during those cold New England winters.

Once, I decided to drive the hay bailer. I drove over with five other guys. Mr. Dee sat in the truck bed and handled the bailer. It would put the loose hay in a square bundle and we'd stack it up later. On each side was two hay pitchers with pitchforks. They'd say, "one two, three," and throw the hay from their pitch forks onto the truck for Mr. Dee to rake up and put into the bailer.

One day, I guess I got bored with all of this and decided to play a trick on all of them. I knew I'd get it in the end from them but I had to do it anyway. Remember, I was young and could be stupid at times.

I told Mr. Dee to hang on! At the sound of one, two, three when the four guys threw the hay high up to land in the truck bed, I jerked the truck forward and all the hay they had thrown up missed! When they all started yelling at me, I backed up on top of the hay so they couldn't get at it to lift it up again.

I yelled out the window, "Make up your minds!" I was laughing inside the truck cab the whole time. Mr. Dee held on to the side of the truck for dear life and said, "Oh, Slick, you done it again." I made sure he was ok though, I loved that old guy.

After doing this about three or four times, all four guys rushed my truck cab. They began to pound on the windows and I played stupid. I shrugged my shoulders and said, "Guys, just quit belly aching and do your job."

Eventually, I had to stop to go to the bathroom. When I went to get out of the cab, they all grabbed me and yanked me to the ground.

They put hay down my pants and everywhere else you can imagine. I was laughing the whole time. They began to laugh with me too. "Valentini, you wise ass." I heard them say. Mr. Dee slowly took off his hat, rubbed his head and smiled.

They never let me drive the hay bailer again.

QUEBECERS, CANUCKS AND BLUENOSERS

For many of us who lived in the New England states, Canada, especially the Maritime Provinces and Quebec didn't seem like a foreign country but more like other neighboring states.

Working at Rocky Neck I'd see a lot of Canadian license plates, mostly those from Quebec with "La Belle Province" stamped on the bottom. I took French class in high school but didn't do that well I must admit. That didn't stop me from trying to converse with the Quebecers or try to pick up on what they were talking about but without much success.

As with the Maritime Canadians from New Brunswick and the Bluenosers from Nova Scotia, all spoke Canadian accented English. I thought they were called Bluenosers because the Maritime Provinces can be very cold, nothing derogatory, just a funny nickname. I've since found out that the term "Bluenose" means someone who is prudish or puritanical. I found people from New Brunswick and Nova Scotia to be nothing of the sort, generally warm and friendly and happy to be swimming in the warm, summer Gulf Stream ocean water of Long Island Sound. "You like this water too, aye?" they asked. These Bluenosers were as fun to listen to as the people from Quebec with the French accent. "Oui Monsieur?"

Our Canadian neighbors were all great people, very polite and never left a mess either on the beach or in the campground for us to clean. I remember visiting Canada as a young child and remarking seeing common citizens picking up refuse lying in the road or on the sidewalk. Canada always seemed to be very clean.

The Canadians were very pleasant people but some had one habit when leaving the beach. This was very different to what New Englanders did or different to what the rest of the United States would do even now I imagine.

When they left the beach, before going to their cars, they took an outside shower to wash off the salt water like the rest of us. The only difference was that when they took a shower outside, they disrobed and stood there in the nude! Obviously their social norms and ours were very dissimilar to say the least. Their idea of public nudity, was very European versus ours that came from a Puritanical past where modesty was the norm. But after all I thought, what was the problem, weren't we all born naked?

We'd laugh at them and say, "Mais non! Non sans slip de bain." But No! Not without a bathing suit.

They'd laugh at us and say, "Dans une minute." In a minute. It wasn't younger aged males or females who showered outside nude but mostly older men and women and they seemed very comfortable in the nude.

The park rangers would get wind of this going on and have a fit. First a large crowd would gather by the outside shower area and by then we all knew what was happening. Fat Freddie hated these antics of our northern neighbors.

Freddie would shout, "Valentini, get some people and hold up a curtain of those tarps to give these damn people some privacy and ask them if they can keep their clothes on!" I was happy to oblige the request. "Allons-y!" Let's go.

These Canadians, mostly from Quebec as they spoke only French, could have showered inside the bathhouse but most of them seemed to enjoy showering outside in the sun. Again, it was mostly older people who didn't seem shy about showering nude outside in public.

All four or five of us faced outward holding up the tarps to prevent the general public from taking pictures with their little Kodak Instamatic Cameras. I took it upon myself to peek over the tarp to make sure everything was okay. I was young and just a little curious.

At just the yell, "Those Canucks are at it again!" sent us running to see this unusual display of public nudity and I loved to watch our park rangers become unnerved by it all. Quickly up went the tarps!

It would be all over too soon, because for the Quebecois, it was just a quick rinse and then the crowd would disperse in about two minutes. Fat Freddie would take his stogie out of his mouth and say, "OK folks, the show is over, go back to the beach."

Finishing up, we'd laugh among ourselves and shake our heads while folding the tarps up. Privately, I always admired French Canadians for just treating showering outside in the nude as part of a normal trip to the beach. "Oh mon Dieu!" Oh my God! I would tell the park rangers with a smile on my face. The rangers in turn would just grunt, turn around and meander off.

This public display of brief nudity didn't really happen that often. It was usually during the week when the beachgoers were sparse and there was a lot more privacy. But still the action we maintenance workers had to take, like holding up the tarps, was a fun break from our normal daily mundane tasks of dumping garbage cans, picking up campground debris or cleaning outhouses. It even put a big grin on the faces of Melvin and Eddie.

When driving a maintenance truck around Rocky Neck, if I spotted a Canadian license plate or mainly one from Quebec, I'd think, oh cool, here we go with another potential show.

We loved all those Canadian folks; neat, polite and some showered nude, without fright.

"Au revoir mes amis!" Goodbye my friends!

TRIBUTE TO MY FELLOW *NUTMEGGAS*

Although we all worked very hard and sometimes the work could be very grueling, I never heard very many complaints about the jobs we had to do, either from the men or the women.

We had a camaraderie of shared experiences, similar to what people share in the military. I developed the work ethic that helped me later in life, to have the stamina to do many jobs, like when I worked seventy-two hour shifts in the military as a war skill medic.

All of us were proud to be part of the park service and to keep the park clean, in working order, and ready for everyone who visited to enjoy.

These parks represented our state of Connecticut, the Nutmeg State, as it was known to us then. These places weren't just mine, or yours but are parks shared by all. We were proud of Rocky Neck State Park and treated it as our own.

When I remember all of the hard work we did to keep the parks presentable, I get disgusted when I go there now for a visit and see garbage sometimes strewn about. I know some of it is the mess caused by seagulls, which we sometimes referred to as flying rats, but mostly I figure is caused by humans.

Perhaps these are people who have never picked up after themselves, have never done any public service or have no civic pride.

That's why today, when I go to visit our state parks, I always pick up whatever I see lying on the ground that should be in the garbage. I pick up the cans, assorted litter and of course those awful disposable baby diapers that are usually left in the parking lots. Where do people think these items will go to and how will they be disposed of?

I also do it out of respect for all those men and women I worked with so long ago, refusing to disparage their dedicated efforts. They were so very proud of their parks and Connecticut, and so am I.

A clean park is a happy park for all to enjoy! Please help keep it that way. Thanks.

Remember Mr. Royal, Al, Melvin, Eddie, Tom, Bob and Mr. Dee are watching you . . . me too.

Overlooking Rocky Neck walking from the pavilion
10/2022 with the crowds gone!

THE TALE OF THE PENNY

Entering the end of those summer days at the park in 1971 and with what I knew was nearly my last day, I was feeling both happy and sad at the same time. I don't know how else to explain it. I remember it was in September and I had to get on with my studies at Western Connecticut State College in Danbury to be a future teacher.

When I worked that last day with Mr. Dee, we didn't talk much and I hate goodbyes. The day ended with us doing our last cleanup and mowing chores. After we put our tools and mowers into the garage by the maintenance room, a plan I had been thinking of for quite a while, began to hatch. I checked the chart that showed the area Mr. Dee would be working at and mowing the following day. Pretty soon the other employees filed in getting ready to head to their cars.

Melvin, Eddie, Al, Fred and others; the whole gang. I shook their hands and they wished me luck at school and said they hoped to see me next year.

I gave Mr. Dee a shoulder hug and said I would see him soon and to have a good off-season at the park.

I quickly drove that clunker MGB over to the nearest bank. I went up to the cashier and got five dollars in pennies, ten coin rolls. I excitedly tore them open and went through them, picking out the shiniest among all of them. I went back and forth to the teller until she got tired of me and said she had other duties. I catch on fast and got the message that it was time for me to depart from the bank.

I had about four hundred really new, flashy, pennies that gleamed in my old glass mayonnaise jar as I drove home. Excited wasn't the word I felt, I was giddy and nervous at the same time with my plan.

Very early the next morning I drove over to Rocky Neck, about four miles away. Looking around to make sure no one was watching, I went to all of the places Mr. Dee would be mowing that day and all the other places we had worked together in years past.

With tears starting to well up in my eyes, I started throwing those pennies all over the fields! Then I started laughing. I put pennies on the out-cropping stone boulders, top of the fences and on all the posts I could find. I could just see his face. See him again, stop, take his straw hat off, rub his bald head and smile. He'd say, "Oh, Slick, you did it now."

He must have had a literal field day in that field. With so many pennies to get, I bet he just stopped working that day. I hope it made him happy. And boy, would he have a pennies tale to tell all the maintenance guys that day at lunch!

I never saw Mr. Dee again and for that matter anyone else who ever worked there. I don't know why that was. I guess my life moved on. The following year I worked at a city park, Ocean Beach Park in New London, working for Frank, the man who controlled all the concession stands at Rocky Neck. I was a bartender and waiter there, but that's another story that remains to be told.

The park's first ranger, Mr. Royal, a man I respected and admired, finally retired that same year that I left in 1971, but it wasn't because of me! He left the park in great order as it was his pride and joy.

When I visit the park, I can still feel his strong willed presence and visualize him coming around a corner, wearing his Smokey Bear hat. He certainly didn't put up with any beach or campground nonsense.

I thought about all those people at Rocky Neck from time to time, when I was building something or if I was doing some type work either as an employee, when I was in the Air Force or as a teacher. They all made me a better person, a harder worker and I can't thank them enough.

Janice too, comes to mind when I see the exit for Rocky Neck and I hope she had a wonderful life and if she or anyone from that time reads this will have a good laugh for old time's sake. I hope no one has dunked her in the ocean lately.

As the Amtrak train winds its way past Rocky Neck and I look out and see everything as if time has stood still. I knew I had to write this all down while my memory is still as bright as a new penny and before my brain oxidizes with each passing year.

Remember, if you find a penny at Rocky Neck, pick it up, make a wish and think of me and Mr. Dee. If it's heads or tails your good fate won't fail. If you have a chance throw out an extra penny, do it. Pass on the good fortune to someone else and return again safely to Rocky Neck, my favorite beach of all time.

Remember, as Mr. Dee would say, "Pennies are a start."

Rich atop the pavilion, at Rocky Neck 10/2022

So, don't delay, take your family out on a lark,
Go fish, swim and camp at this place, your park.
Pack up your cars, set out for a trek,
Visit the place that I love, it's called Rocky Neck.

Rich Valentini

ACKNOWLEDGEMENTS

I'd like to thank all of the people who have helped make this memoir possible: Amy and Carolyn, current employees from Rocky Neck State Park, Liz from Staples in Old Saybrook, CT., Cassie, Christopher and Anthony from Staples in Yuba City, CA.

The people at Friesen Publishing, especially Jamie Olliver and Benjamin Fligg.

Also, I want to thank Charlie from Young's Village in Madison, CT for his professional and mentoring knowledge, to my friends and other teachers who helped with editing suggestions and of course to Alice, my wife, for her continued support.

And lastly to Bob, Eddie, Fred, Janice, Melvin, Mr. Dee, Mr. Royal and Tom and to the rest of those former employees at Rocky Neck for putting up with my antics and for giving me the lifelong inspiration to finally write all of this down. Again, thanks for so many life lessons. I miss you all.

Rich Valentini

CPSIA information can be obtained
at www.ICGtesting.com
Printed in the USA
BVHW060452060323
659613BV00005B/16